*Every snowflake is a package of holiday Blessings*

# Say *It With* Style

## Inspired Quotes for Every Card-Making Occasion

*Health to you*

*Wealth to you and the Best that*

*Life*

*can give you*

**EDITED BY TANYA FOX**

*you are priceless*

*shredded money*

*a little bird told me*

HOUSE of
WHITE
BIRCHES
PUBLISHERS
SINCE 1947

# Say *It With* Style 2

| | |
|---:|:---|
| **EDITOR** | Tanya Fox |
| **ART DIRECTOR** | Brad Snow |
| **PUBLISHING SERVICES DIRECTOR** | Brenda Gallmeyer |
| **ASSOCIATE EDITOR** | Brooke Smith |
| **ASSISTANT ART DIRECTOR** | Nick Pierce |
| **COPY SUPERVISOR** | Deborah Morgan |
| **COPY EDITORS** | Amanda Scheerer, Emily Carter |
| **TECHNICAL EDITOR** | Corene Painter |
| **PHOTOGRAPHY SUPERVISOR** | Tammy Christian |
| **PHOTOGRAPHY STYLISTS** | Tammy Liechty, Tammy Steiner |
| **PHOTOGRAPHY** | Matthew Owen |
| **PRODUCTION ARTIST SUPERVISOR** | Erin Augsburger |
| **GRAPHIC ARTIST** | Nicole Gage |
| **PRODUCTION ASSISTANTS** | Marj Morgan, Judy Neuenschwander |

Printed in USA
First Printing: 2011
Library of Congress Control Number: 2010911416
ISBN: 978-1-59635-347-3

AnniesAttic.com

1  2  3  4  5  6  7  8  9

Every effort has been made to ensure that the instructions in this publication are complete and accurate.
We cannot, however, take responsibility for human error, typographical mistakes or variations in individual work.
Please visit AnniesCustomerCare.com to check for pattern updates.

# WELCOME

Dear crafting friend,

I believe I can now classify myself as a quotation collector. This new hobby, if you will, began a few years back when I was working on our first collection of quotes. I was gripped by the powerful words that have been spoken over time; words that inspire, encourage, make us laugh and others that cause us to pause and ponder their true meaning. From that time until now, I've archived every quote that I've come across, knowing that someday the perfect occasion would arise to use it in a handcrafted greeting card or memory page.

It is with great pleasure that we present a second volume of quotes that have been carefully selected for your crafting pleasure. Sentiments and expressions to cover every imaginable card-making occasion have been conveniently arranged by occasions listed in alphabetical order. Whether you're looking for a snappy card sentiment for your best girlfriend's birthday, a snippet of wisdom for the graduate or newly married couple, or a creative headline for a treasured scrapbook page, you'll find just what you need right here among the more than 1,100 quotes that fill these pages.

When you need just the right words to express what you feel, let *Say It With Style 2* be your guide.

*Tanya*

*Most collectors collect tangibles. As a quotation collector, I collect wisdom, life, invisible beauty, souls alive in ink.*

—Terri Guillemets

# CONTENTS

*No matter what anybody tells you,
words and ideas can change the world.*

—Robin Williams, *Dead Poet's Society*

# Fill your paper with the breathings of your heart.

—William Wordsworth

# Birthdays

May God bless your birthday
With blessings from above,
Fill it full of sunshine,
And wrap it up in love!

y God bl      essings f
ove, fill it              it up in
d bless y               ngs from

And in the end, it's not the years in your life that count. It's the life in your years.

—Abraham Lincoln

"Over the hill" is a relative term —but here's a sled, just in case. Happy Birthday!

As God adds life to your years, may He add years to your life. Happy Birthday!

A birthday only happens once in a lifetime. Today, I am celebrating the anniversary of your birth.

*Age does not matter, you can party as much as you want.*

*Age is a number and mine is unlisted.*

—Author Unknown

Although I can't wish you a happy birthday in person, I will spend the whole day with happy thoughts of you.

## Because you're the gift in my life, I give you my gift of love.

Because time itself is like a spiral, something special happens on your birthday each year: The same energy that God invested in you at birth is present once again.

—Menachem Mendel Schneerson

# Birthdays

Cherish God's love and celebrate His plan for you! Happy Birthday!

**Birthdays are ordinary days sprinkled with stardust.**

Birthdays are filled with yesterday's memories, today's joys and tomorrow's dreams.

**Count your life by smiles, not tears. Count your age by friends, not years.**

*Don't count the years, count the blessings.*

Each birthday is a new beginning, full of promise and opportunity and the chance to make dreams come true.

Every year on your birthday, you get a chance to start new.

—Sammy Hagar

Everyone is the age of their heart.

—Guatemalan Proverb

Everything slows down with age, except the time it takes cake and ice cream to reach your hips.

—Attributed to John Wagner

*From morning till night, may your birthday be bright.*

God is so wise that He never created friends with price tags. If He did, I wouldn't have been able to afford a precious friend like you.

Hope lovely surprises are coming your way, to make your birthday a wonderful day.

*Happy birthday to someone who is forever young.*

## Here's to another year of experience.

*I hope all your birthday dreams and wishes come true.*

I hope that for every candle on your cake you get a wonderful surprise.

## Hope your birthday blossoms into lots of dreams come true!

# Birthdays

It is clear that God created you for a great purpose. Happy Birthday!

I thank God for the day that you were born and for you being such a great friend to me.

Lots of people are thinking of you on your birthday; I just wanted to let you know I'm one of them!

*Here's to celebrating you!*

I love everything that's old: old friends, old times, old manners, old books, old wines.

—Oliver Goldsmith

I'm enthralled by your beauty, mesmerized by your charisma and spellbound by your love. No wonder I am always thinking about you.

**It's always nice to wish the best to someone who really is!**

*It's sad to grow old, but nice to ripen.*

—Brigitte Bardot

Just like fine wine, you grow better with the years.

Lying about your age is easier now that
you sometimes forget what it is.

## May this year be your best ever.

*May each and every passing year
bring you wisdom, peace and cheer.*

May God bless your birthday with blessings from above,
fill it full of sunshine and wrap it up in love!

**May this day
bring to you
all things that
make you smile.
Happy Birthday!**

*May today be filled with
sunshine and smiles,
laughter and love.*

Make a wish!

May this birthday be just the beginning
of a year filled with happy memories,
wonderful moments and shining dreams.

# Birthdays

May your spirit keep the freedom of a butterfly in spring, and may your heart be filled always with the joys of simple things.

Not just a year older, but a year better.

*May your birthday be as full of love as you are!*

On your birthday, count your candles, count your years, count your blessings.

*Our birthdays are feathers in the broad wing of time.*

—Jean Paul Richter

Remember, you'll be this age for only one year, but you'll be awesome forever.

## Sorry I forgot the most important day of the year ... your birthday!

The more you praise and celebrate your life, the more there is in life to celebrate.

—Oprah Winfrey

Sorry I forgot your birthday.
Can you reschedule it for sometime next week?

# The most special thing about this card ... is the person holding it.

*The old believe everything, the middle-aged suspect everything, the young know everything.*

—Oscar Wilde

There is always a lot to be thankful for, if you take the time to look. For example, I'm sitting here thinking how nice it is that wrinkles don't hurt.

—Author Unknown

To the world, you may be one person. But to me, you are the world.

*Today is a gift of life, today it's your birthday.*

**Today, take time for you, and enjoy every little thing you do.**

We did not change as we grew older; we just became more clearly ourselves.

—Lynn Hall

Wishing you a year filled with the same joy you bring to others.

# Christmas

WELCOME CHRISTMAS
*Season's Greetings*
INTO YOUR HEART

A Christmas candle is a lovely thing; it makes no noise at all, but softly gives itself away.

—Eva Logue

A little smile, a word of cheer, a bit of love from someone near, a little gift from one held dear, best wishes for the coming year… These make a Merry Christmas!

—John Greenleaf Whittier

A merry Christmas to everybody! A happy new year to all the world!

—Charles Dickens

*As long as we know in our hearts what Christmas ought to be, Christmas is.*

—Eric Sevareid

*At Christmas, all roads lead home.*

—Marjorie Holmes

Christmas comes just once a year, but you're in our hearts all year long.

Blessed is the season which engages the whole world in a conspiracy of love!

—Hamilton Wright Mabie

Bless us Lord, this Christmas, with quietness of mind; teach us to be patient and always to be kind.

—Helen Steiner Rice

**Be naughty and save Santa a trip.**

*Have a jolly Christmas.*

Christmas in Bethlehem. The ancient dream:
A cold, clear night made brilliant by a glorious star,
the smell of incense, shepherds and wise men
falling to their knees in adoration of the sweet baby,
the incarnation of perfect love.

—Lucinda Franks

Christmas is a time of joy, a time for love and cheer,
a time for making memories, to last throughout the year.

*Christmas is a time when you get homesick*
*—even when you're home.*

—Carol Nelson

Christmas, children, is not a date.
It is a state of mind.

—Mary Ellen Chase

Christmas is not as much about opening
our presents as opening our hearts.

—Janice Maeditere

**Christmas waves a magic wand over this world,
and behold, everything is softer and more beautiful.**

—Norman Vincent Peale

Christmas, my child, is love in action.
Every time we love, every time we give,
it's Christmas.

**Let it snow!**

—Dale Evans Rogers

For unto us a child is born, unto us a son is given;
and the government shall be upon his shoulders;
and his name shall be called Wonderful, Counsellor,
the Mighty God, the everlasting Father,
the Prince of Peace.

—Isaiah 9:6 (Kings James Version)

From home to home,
and heart to heart,
from one place to another.
The warmth and joy of Christmas
brings us closer to each other.

**Give the magic of the season.**

—Emily Matthews

*Friends like you put the warmth and good cheer into this special time of year.*

*Have a merrie olde Christmas!*

He who has not Christmas in his heart
will never find it under a tree.

—Roy L. Smith

Home for the holidays.

# Christmas

## Jingle all the way.

## Welcome Christmas into your heart.

Hope this happy season is full of fun surprises.

*I will honor Christmas in my heart, and try to keep it all the year.*

—Charles Dickens

*It's snow time!*

Jesus, the Light of the World, as we celebrate Your birth … may we begin to see the world in the light of understanding You give us.

*Keep the Christmas spirit.*

*I heard the bells on Christmas Day, their old, familiar carols play, and wild and sweet, the word repeat, of peace on earth, good-will to men!*

—Henry Wadsworth Longfellow

*Let's meet under the mistletoe.*

Love came down at Christmas, love all lovely, love divine;
love was born at Christmas; star and angels gave the sign.

—Christina Rossetti

Love is the music of Christmas.

May Christmas be evergreen in your heart.

*May His voice be heard in the quiet stillness of this holy season.*

*May peace and joy abide in your heart now and all year through.*

May peace be your gift at Christmas and your blessing all year through!

—Author Unknown

**May simple gifts bring great joy at Christmas.**

May the Christmas season fill your home with joy, your heart with love and your life with laughter.

# Christmas

May the magic of Christmas touch your heart and home.

**May the gifts of the season be yours now and always.**

May the warmth of your heart draw near at Christmas.

May the spirit of Christmas bring you peace, the gladness of Christmas give you hope, the warmth of Christmas grant you love.

—Author Unknown

May the wonder of this magical season warm your heart and home.

May we not "spend" Christmas or "observe" Christmas, but rather "keep" it.

—Peter Marshall

*May your blessings outnumber the snowflakes this holiday season.*

*May your holidays be filled with peace and joy.*

Never worry about the size of your Christmas tree. In the eyes of children, they are all 30 feet tall.

—Larry Wilde

Our hearts grow tender with childhood memories and love of kindred, and we are better throughout the year for having, in spirit, become a child again at Christmastime.

—Laura Ingalls Wilder

*Peace on earth will come to stay when we live Christmas every day.*

Perhaps the best Yuletide decoration is being wreathed in smiles.

—Author Unknown

**Santa's on his way.**

Jingle bell rock.

*Sing hey! Sing hey! For Christmas Day;*
*twine mistletoe and holly.*
*For a friendship glows in winter snows,*
*and so let's all be jolly!*

—Author Unknown

The true spirit of Christmas is love.

—Linda Willis

This season, the best gift of all is your friendship.

This is the message of Christmas: We are never alone.

—Taylor Caldwell

When the world says, "Give up," HOPE WHISPERS, "Try it one more time."

*A bend in the road is not the end of the road ... unless you fail to make the turn.*

—Author Unknown

Adversity is like a strong wind. It tears away from us all but the things that cannot be torn, so that we see ourselves as we really are.

—Arthur Golden, *Memoirs of a Geisha*

Always be a first-rate version of yourself instead of a second-rate version of somebody else.

—Judy Garland

An inventor fails 999 times, and if he succeeds once, he's in. He treats his failures simply as practice shots.

—Charles F. Kettering

*Every path hath a puddle.*

—George Herbert

Birds sing after a storm; why shouldn't people feel as free to delight in whatever remains to them?

—Rose F. Kennedy

Convert difficulties into opportunities, for difficulties are divine surgeries to make you better.

—Author Unknown

**Faith makes this possible, not easy.**

# Encouragement

Do what you can,
with what you have,
where you are.

—Theodore Roosevelt

*Have the courage to face a difficulty lest it kick you harder than you bargained for.*

—Stanislaus I, Maxims

**How long should you try? Until.**

—Jim Rohn

Don't cry when the sun is gone, because the tears won't let you see the stars.

—Violeta Parra

*Better to do something imperfectly than to do nothing flawlessly.*

—Robert H. Schuller

*Be master of your petty annoyances and conserve your energies for the big, worthwhile things. It isn't the mountain ahead that wears you out—it's the grain of sand in your shoe.*

—Robert Service

Diseases can be our spiritual flat tires—disruptions in our lives that seem to be disasters at the time, but end by redirecting our lives in a meaningful way.

—Bernie S. Siegel

*For with each dawn, she found new hope that someday, her dreams of happiness would come true.*

—*Cinderella*

Good fortune shies away from gloom. Keep your spirits up. Good things will come to you, and you will come to good things.

—Glorie Abelhas

## Happiness can be found, even in the darkest of times, if one only remembers to turn on the light.

—J.K. Rowling, *Harry Potter and the Prisoner of Azkaban*

*If life doesn't offer a game worth playing, invent a new one.*

—Anthony J. D'Angelo

I ask not for a lighter burden, but for broader shoulders.

—Jewish Proverb

Even if the hopes you started out with are dashed, hope has to be maintained.

—Seamus Heaney

I had the blues because I had no shoes until, upon the street, I met a man who had no feet.

—Denis Waitley

# Encouragement

It's only from the valley that the mountain seems high.

*In the depth of winter I finally learned that there was in me an invincible summer.*

—Albert Camus

Make failure your teacher, not your undertaker.

—Zig Ziglar

**Light always follows darkness.**

*Don't wish it were easier, wish you were better.*
*Don't wish for fewer problems, wish for more skills.*
*Don't wish for less challenges, wish for more wisdom.*

—Earl Shoaf

Even a happy life cannot be without a measure of darkness, and the word happy would lose its meaning if it were not balanced by sadness.

—Carl Jung

Don't duck the most difficult problems.
That just ensures that the hardest part will
be left when you are most tired.
Get the big one done; it's downhill from then on.

—Norman Vincent Peale

Holding on to anger, resentment and hurt only gives you tense muscles, a headache and a sore jaw from clenching your teeth. Forgiveness gives you back the laughter and the lightness in your life.

—Joan Lunden

Hope begins in the dark, the stubborn hope that if you just show up and try to do the right thing, the dawn will come.

—Anne Lamott

I am only one, but I am one. I cannot do everything, but I can do something. And I will not let what I cannot do interfere with what I can do.

—Edward Everett Hale

*It's not easy taking my problems one at a time when they refuse to get in line.*

—Ashleigh Brilliant

Life is a shipwreck but we must not forget to sing in the lifeboats.

—Voltaire

*Never place a period where God has placed a comma.*

—George Burns

Life isn't about waiting for the storm to pass, it's about learning to dance in the rain.

Smooth seas do not make a skillful sailor.

—African Proverb

Only those who are asleep make no mistakes.

—Ingvar Kamprad

*The greater the obstacle, the more glory in overcoming it.*

—Moliére

The difficulties of life are intended to make us better, not bitter.

I have sometimes been wildly, despairingly, acutely miserable, but through it all I still know quite certainly that just to be alive is a grand thing.

—Agatha Christie

**I know God will not give me anything I can't handle. I just wish that He didn't trust me so much.**

—Mother Teresa

If one dream should fall and break into a thousand pieces, never be afraid to pick one of those pieces up and begin again.

—Flavia Weedn

*If you don't like something change it; if you can't change it, change the way you think about it.*

—Maya Angelou

## I've developed a new philosophy ... I only dread one day at a time.

— Charlie Brown in Charles Schultz' comic *Peanuts*

May the light always find you on a dreary day.
When you need to be home, may you find your way.
May you always have courage to take a chance.
And never find frogs in your underpants.

—An Irish toast

No life is so hard that you can't make
it easier by the way you take it.

—Ellen Glasgow

*The human spirit is stronger than anything that can happen to it.*

—C.C. Scott

To be upset over what you don't have is to waste what you do have.

—Ken S. Keyes Jr.

To be wronged is nothing, unless you continue to remember it.

—Confucius

## Turn your wounds into wisdom.

—Oprah Winfrey

# Encouragement

We must embrace pain and burn it as fuel for our journey.

—Kenji Miyazawa

The art of living lies less in eliminating our troubles than in growing with them.

—Bernard M. Baruch

**You always pass failure on the way to success.**

—Mickey Rooney

We are like tea bags—we don't know our own strength until we're in hot water.

—Sister Busche

*Only one principle will give you courage—that is the principle that no evil lasts forever nor indeed for very long.*

—Epicurus

People seldom see the halting and painful steps by which the most insignificant success is achieved.

—Anne Sullivan

Perhaps all the dragons of our lives are princesses who are only waiting to see us once beautiful and brave.

—Rainer Maria Rilke

Sometimes in tragedy we find our life's purpose— the eye sheds a tear to find its focus.

—Robert Brault

Things turn out best for the people who make the best out of the way things turn out.

—Art Linkletter

To achieve anything in this game you must be prepared to dabble in the boundary of disaster.

—Sterling Moss

When it is obvious that the goals cannot be reached, don't adjust the goals, adjust the action steps.

—Confucius

When the world says, "Give up," hope whispers, "Try it one more time."

When written in Chinese the word "crisis" is composed of two characters—one represents danger and the other represents opportunity.

—John F. Kennedy

You can learn little from victory. You can learn everything from defeat.

—Christy Mathewson

**You must be at the end of your rope. I felt a tug.**

—Author Unknown

While we may not be able to control all that happens to us, we can control what happens inside us.

—Benjamin Franklin

Family

ck I know                      nly instit
works is                       I know t
only insti                     s is the f

FAMILY
FOREVER

A babe in the house is a wellspring of pleasure, a messenger of peace and love, a resting place for innocence on earth, a link between angels and men.

—Martin Farquhar Tupper

A baby has a special way of adding joy in every single day.

—Author Unknown

A baby is an inestimable blessing and bother.

—Mark Twain

*A baby is sunshine and moonbeams and more brightening your world as never before.*

—Author Unknown

A baby will make love stronger, days shorter, nights longer, bankroll smaller, home happier, clothes shabbier, the past forgotten and the future worth living for.

—Anonymous

A boy is a magical creature—you can lock him out of your workshop, but you can't lock him out of your heart.

—Allan Beck

**A baby's smile melts the heart and calms the soul.**

A daughter is a day brightener and a heart warmer.

—Author Unknown

# Family

A son is a son till he takes him a wife, a daughter is a daughter all of her life.

—Irish Saying

*A sweet new blossom of humanity.*

—Author Unknown

**Children make you want to start life over.**

—Muhammad Ali

Children are the hands by which we take hold of heaven.

—Henry Ward Beecher

*A daughter is a gift of love.*

—Author Unknown

A daughter is the happy memories of the past, the joyful moments of the present, and the hope and promise of the future.

—Author Unknown

*A daughter may outgrow your lap, but she will never outgrow your heart.*

—Author Unknown

A little girl is sugar and spice and everything nice— especially when she's taking a nap.

—Author Unknown

A three-year-old child is a being who gets almost
as much fun out of a $56 set of swings as it
does out of finding a small green worm.

—Bill Vaughan

Any kid will run any errand for
you if you ask at bedtime.

—Red Skelton

Anyone who thinks the art of conversation is
dead ought to tell a child to go to bed.

—Robert Gallagher

*Children need Love, especially
when they do not deserve it.*

—Harold Hulbert

**Children reinvent your world for you.**

—Susan Sarandon

It is not a slight
thing when those
so fresh from
God love us.

—Charles Dickens

Kids: They
dance before
they learn there
is anything that
isn't music.

—William Stafford

*Family Forever*

# Family

*Sweet little angel face lifts me up with just a gaze.*

## Son, you outgrew my lap, but never my heart.

—Author Unknown

The only thing worth stealing is a kiss from a sleeping child.

—Joe Houldsworth

*Straight from heaven up above, here is a baby for us to love.*

It sometimes happens, even in the best of families, that a baby is born. This is not necessarily cause for alarm. The important thing is to keep your wits about you and borrow some money.

—Elinor Goulding Smith

Every child comes with the message that God is not yet discouraged of man.

—Rabindranath Tagore

*Having a child is surely the most beautifully irrational act that two people in love can commit.*

—Bill Cosby

## No one likes change but babies in diapers.

—Barbara Johnson

Every child born into the world is a new thought of God, an ever-fresh and radiant possibility.

—Kate Douglas Wiggin

Loving a baby is a circular business, a kind of feedback loop. The more you give the more you get and the more you get the more you feel like giving.

—Penelope Leac

Nothing you do for children is ever wasted.
They seem not to notice us, hovering, averting
our eyes, and they seldom offer thanks,
but what we do for them is never wasted.

—Garrison Keillor

*A friend is a brother who was once a bother.*

—Author Unknown

**To a father growing old nothing is dearer than a daughter.**

—Euripides

A brother shares childhood memories and grown-up dreams.

—Author Unknown

*You are my sonshine.*

—Author Unknown

A sister shares childhood memories and grown-up dreams.

—Author Unknown

*And thank you for a house full of people I love. Amen.*

—Terri Guillemets

*A sister is a little bit of childhood that can never be lost.*

—Marion C. Garretty

Ten fingers, 10 toes.
She's laughter and teardrops,
so small and brand new,
and amazingly angelic,
she's sent to bless you,
she's one special baby,
the best of life's treasure,
and will grant and bless you,
many hours of great pleasure.

—Author Unknown

While we try to teach our children all about life, our children teach us what life is all about.

—Angela Schwindt

The spirit is there in every boy; it has to be discovered and brought to light.

—Sir Robert Baden-Powell

*Watching your daughter being collected by her date feels like handing over a million dollar Stradivarius to a gorilla.*

—Jim Bishop

A sibling may be the keeper of one's identity, the only person with the keys to one's unfettered, more fundamental self.

—Marian Sandmaier

A sister can be seen as someone who is both ourselves and very much not ourselves—a special kind of double.

—Toni Morrison

A sister is a gift to the heart, a friend to the spirit, a golden thread to the meaning of life.

—Isadora James

A sister smiles when one tells one's stories—for she knows where the decoration has been added.

—Chris Montaigne

In the cookies of life, sisters are the chocolate chips.

—Author Unknown

In time of test, family is best.

—Burmese proverb

It is not flesh and blood, but the heart which makes us fathers and sons.

—Johann Schiller

Is solace anywhere more comforting than that in the arms of a sister.

—Alice Walker

# Family

**Our roots say we're sisters, our hearts say we're friends.**

—Author Unknown

Our brothers and sisters are there with us from the dawn of our personal stories to the inevitable dusk.

—Susan Scarf Merrell

More than Santa Claus, your sister knows when you've been bad and good.

—Linda Sunshine

**Brothers and sisters are as close as hands and feet.**

—Vietnamese Proverb

Call it a clan, call it a network, call it a tribe, call it a family. Whatever you call it, whoever you are, you need one.

—Jane Howard

I sought my soul, but my soul I could not see.
I sought my God, but my God eluded me.
I sought my brother and I found all three.

—Author Unknown

It was nice growing up with someone like you—someone to lean on, someone to count on ... someone to tell on!

—Author Unknown

*Our siblings. They resemble us just enough to make all their differences confusing, and no matter what we choose to make of this, we are cast in relation to them our whole lives long.*

—Susan Scarf Merrell

The only rock I know that stays steady, the only institution I know that works is the family.

—Lee Iacocca

Sisters are blossoms in the garden of life.

—Author Unknown

*Sisterhood is powerful.*

—Robin Morgan

**Sometimes being a brother is even better than being a superhero.**

—Marc Brown

Sisters share the scent and smells—the feel of a common childhood.

—Pam Brown

Friendship

Friends are special treasures of the heart!

A friend is someone who can see through
you but still enjoys the show.

—Author Unknown

A friend is someone who understands your past,
believes in your future and
accepts you just the way you are.

*A friend knows the song in my heart and
sings it to me when my memory fails.*

—Donna Roberts

A friend may well be reckoned the
masterpiece of nature.

—Ralph Waldo Emerson

## A true friend can hear a tear drop.

A true friend unbosoms
freely, advises justly,
assists readily, adventures
boldly, takes all patiently,
defends courageously
and continues a friend
unchangeably.

—William Penn

A friend is the one
who walks in when
others walk out.

—Walter Winchell

A true friend never gets
in your way unless you
happen to be going down.

—Arnold H. Glasow

# Friendship

**Friends are God's way of taking care of us.**

Friends are special treasures of the heart!

*Friendship warms the heart.*

Friendship is unnecessary, like philosophy, like art. ... It has no survival value; rather it is one of those things that give value to survival.

—C. S. Lewis

*But friendship is precious, not only in the shade, but in the sunshine of life, and thanks to a benevolent arrangement the greater part of life is sunshine.*

—Thomas Jefferson

Don't walk in front of me, I may not follow. Don't walk behind me, I may not lead. Just walk beside me and be my friend.

—Albert Carnus

Friends ... they cherish one another's hopes. They are kind to one another's dreams.

—Henry David Thoreau

*Friends are for sharing hearts.*

*Good friends are like quilts—they age with you yet never lose their warmth.*

*Good friends are the rare jewels of life—difficult to find and impossible to replace.*

Hold a true friend with both your hands.

—Nigerian Proverb

I awoke this morning with devout thanksgiving for my friends, the old and the new.

—Ralph Waldo Emerson

## I get by with a little help from my friends.

—John Lennon

I value the friend who for me finds time on his calendar, but I cherish the friend who for me does not consult his calendar.

—Robert Brault

I have friends in overalls whose friendship I would not swap for the favor of the kings of the world.

—Thomas A. Edison

My thoughts are free to go anywhere, but it's surprising how often they head in your direction.

## If friends are flowers, we must be best buds!

# Friendship

The language of friendship is not words but meanings.

—Henry David Thoreau

Lots of people want to ride with you in the limo, but what you want is someone who will take the bus with you when the limo breaks down.

—Oprah Winfrey

*Search not for a friend in time of need, for a true friend shall find thee.*

—Author Unknown

If instead of a gem, or even a flower, we should cast the gift of a loving thought into the heart of a friend, that would be giving as the angels give.

—George MacDonald

If you have an ounce of common sense and one good friend, you don't need an analyst.

—Joan Crawford

If you live to be a hundred, I want to live to be a hundred minus one day, so I never have to live without you.

—Winnie the Pooh

In everyone's life, at some time, our inner fire goes out. It is then burst into flame by an encounter with another human being. We should all be thankful for those people who rekindle the inner spirit.

—Albert Schweitzer

Silences make the real conversations between friends.
Not the saying but the never needing to say is what counts.

—Margaret Lee Runbeck

The most beautiful discovery true friends make is that
they can grow separately without growing apart.

—Elisabeth Foley

*The most I can do for my friend
is simply to be his friend.*

—Henry David Thoreau

## There is nothing on this earth more to be prized than true friendship.

—St. Thomas Aquinas

To have one true friend is lucky,
to have a friend like you is a miracle.

Walking with a
friend in the dark is
better than walking
alone in the light.

—Helen Keller

*True friendship
isn't about being
there when it's
convenient; it's
about being there
when it's not.*

# Get Well

...hugs and prayers
from someone who cares.

A bad cold wouldn't be so annoying if it weren't for the advice of our friends.

—Kin Hubbard

A smile, a puppy, the rainbow after a storm— some happy thoughts sent your way in hopes that you feel better soon.

*A sunbeam to warm you, a moonbeam to charm you, a sheltering angel, so nothing can harm you.*

—Irish Blessing

Ask any child and they'll tell you that a bandage makes everything feel better.

## Attitudes are contagious. Are yours worth catching?

—Dennis and Wendy Mannering

Being in a good frame of mind helps keep one in the picture of health.

—Author Unknown

*...hugs and prayers from someone who cares.*

Bandage solutions have been given a bad name. They help keep things from getting worse while other forces are at work making things better.

# Get Well

## Happy Healing!

Hoping that with each new day brings more strength, brighter days and bigger smiles. Get well soon.

Life is not merely to be alive, but to be well.

—Marcus Valerius Martial

*Being sick isn't easy but I hope it makes it easier knowing that others are thinking of you and sending well wishes your way.*

Comfy jammies, cozy bed,
big soft pillow for your head.
Worry not, the world can wait,
take your time and recuperate.

**Hope you perk up soon!**

For every day that there is sunshine, there will be days of rain, it's how we dance within them both that shows our love and pain.

—Joey Tolbert

Good fortune shies away from gloom.
Keep your spirits up. Good things will come
to you and you will come to good things.

—Glorie Abelhas

He will cover you with His feathers, and under
His wings you will find refuge; His faithfulness
will be your shield and rampart.

—Psalm 91:4 (New International Version)

I enjoy convalescence. It is the part
that makes the illness worthwhile.

—George Bernard Shaw

I know I can't take away or lessen unhealthy physical
symptoms, but, what I can do is tell my best wishes for
you on your road to recovery is always on my mind.

—Byron Pulsifer

## Pain, pain go away!

Our office just doesn't
run as smoothly
without you, please
get well soon.

*May you find
comfort knowing that
your restored health
is our greatest wish.*

May each day bring
you renewed strength
and brighter times.

# Get Well

The I in illness is isolation, and the crucial letters in wellness are we.

—Author Unknown

*The gift of time and rest may be the best get-well gift of all. Make sure to give yourself that gift.*

I learned a long time ago that minor surgery is when they do the operation on someone else, not you.

—Bill Walton

*If knowing that someone cares helps the healing process ... then you should be feeling better already.*

If your body's not right, the rest of your day will go all wrong. Take care of yourself.

—Terri Guillemets

**Not all healing comes from the doctor's hands or from the medicine. We are praying for your full recovery.**

Say you are well, or all is well with you, and God shall hear your words and make them true.

—Ella Wheeler Wilcox

*Sending a little sunshine, to sprinkle in your day, reminding you that you're thought of, in a warm and special way!*

The office is too quiet without your laughter, the clock seems to tick slower, and the plants are starting to droop without your sunny face to cheer them. Please get better soon!

There is no medicine like hope, no incentive so great and no tonic so powerful as expectation of something tomorrow.

—Orison Swett Marden

*Thinking of you and hoping you're up and about soon!*

**Time is the best doctor.**

—Yiddish Proverb

Until the sun comes out again for you, my umbrella is big enough for two.

Think of nothing other than what you need to heal; everything else is secondary.

# Holidays

the promise ... ith peace
joy. May the ... you wit
ce and joy. M ... ster fill y

May the promise
of Easter
fill you with
peace & joy.

As we start the new year, let's get down on our knees to thank God we're on our feet.

—Irish Toast

Cheers to a new year and another chance for us to get it right.

—Oprah Winfrey

Good resolutions are simply checks that men draw on a bank where they have no account.

—Oscar Wilde

*Let us resolve to do the best we can with what we've got.*

—William Feather

*May all your troubles last as long as your New Year's resolutions.*

—Joey Adams

## New Year's Day is every man's birthday.

—Charles Lamb

An optimist stays up until midnight to see the new year in. A pessimist stays up to make sure the old year leaves.

—Bill Vaughan

The object of a new year is not that we should have a new year. It is that we should have a new soul.

—G.K. Chesterton

Year's end is neither an end nor a beginning, but a going on with all the wisdom that experience can instill in us.

—Hal Borland

*You're my pot of gold!*

St. Patrick's Day is an enchanted time—a day to begin transforming winter's dreams into summer's magic.

—Adrienne Cook

If you hold a four-leaf shamrock in your left hand at dawn on St. Patrick's Day, you get what you want very much but haven't wished for.

—Patricia Lynch

May the Irish hills caress you.
May her lakes and rivers bless you.
May the luck of the Irish enfold you.
May the blessings of Saint Patrick behold you.

May the leprechauns dance over your bed
and bring you sweet dreams.
May you always walk in sunshine.
May you never want for more.
May Irish angels rest their wings
right beside your door.

*For each petal on the shamrock, this brings a wish your way, good health, good luck and happiness for today and every day.*

For I remember it is Easter morn, and life and love and peace are all new born.

—Alice Freeman Palmer

*Hippity hoppity, Easter's on its way!*

*Let the resurrection joy lift us from loneliness and weakness and despair to strength and beauty and happiness.*

—Floyd W. Tomkins

May the promise of Easter fill you with peace and joy.

On Easter Day, the veil between time and eternity thins to gossamer.

—Douglas Horton

## Some bunny loves you!

Another egg-scuse for chocolate!

Easter is the only time it's safe to put all your eggs in one basket!

Bunnies are cuddly, the large and the small. But I like chocolate ones best of all.

*Celebrate freedom!*

**Democracy is the government of the people, by the people, for the people.**

—Abraham Lincoln

Happy birthday, America!

**Celebrate the 4th!**

A man's country is not a certain area of land, of mountains, rivers and woods, but it is a principle; and patriotism is loyalty to that principle.

—George William Curtis

America, for me, has been the pursuit and catching of happiness.

—Aurora Raigne

America is a passionate idea or it is nothing. America is a human brotherhood or it is chaos.

—Max Lerner

*America is a tune. It must be sung together.*

—Gerald Stanley Lee

America is much more than a geographical fact. It is a political and moral fact—the first community in which men set out in principle to institutionalize freedom, responsible government and human equality.

—Adlai Stevenson

And so, my fellow Americans: ask not what your country can do for you—ask what you can do for your country. My fellow citizens of the world: ask not what America will do for you, but what together we can do for the freedom of man.

—John F. Kennedy

*I love my freedom.*
*I love my America.*

—Jessi Lane Adams

**Freedom is nothing else but a chance to be better.**

—Albert Camus

*Patriotism is easy to understand in America—it means looking out for yourself by looking out for your country.*

—Calvin Coolidge

Liberty is the breath of life to nations.

—George Bernard Shaw

When witches go riding,
and black cats are seen,
the moon laughs and whispers,
" 'tis near Halloween."

—Author Unknown

Clothes make a statement.
Costumes tell a story.

—Mason Coole

Ghosts, like ladies,
never speak
till spoke to.

—Richard Harris Barham

**Have a fang-tastic night!**

On Halloween,
The witches fly, across the sky,
the owls go "Who? Who? Who?"
The black cats yowl, and green ghosts howl
"Scary Halloween to you!"

—Nina Willis Walter

Pumpkins on a fence post, with their eyes alight,
bats and cats and hooty owls, witches all in flight,
ghosts and goblins galloping, what a scary night!

—Author Unknown

*Shadows of a thousand years rise again unseen,*
*voices whisper in the trees "Tonight is Halloween!"*

—Dexter Kozen

A thankful heart is not only the greatest virtue, but the parent of all other virtues.

—Cicero

Forever on Thanksgiving Day, the heart will find the pathway home.

—Wilbur D. Nesbit

Give this one day to thanks, to joy, to gratitude.

—Henry Ward Beecher

Gratitude is born in hearts that take time to count up past mercies.

—Charles E. Jefferson

**Gratitude is the sign of noble souls.**

—Aesop

Thanksgiving was never meant to be shut up in a single day.

—Robert Caspar Lintner

Let us come before His presence with thanksgiving, and make a joyful noise unto Him with psalms.

This is the finest measure of thanksgiving: a thankfulness that springs from love.

—William C. Skeath

Thanksgiving, after all, is a word of action.

—W.J. Cameron

# Inspirational

Keep your face to the **sunshine** & you cannot see the shadow.
HELEN KELLER

A mind once stretched by a new idea never regains its original dimensions.

—Oliver Wendell Holmes

A ship in harbor is safe, but that is not what ships are built for.

—John A. Shedd

Always do right. This will gratify some people and astonish the rest.

—Mark Twain

Always think outside the box and embrace opportunities that appear, wherever they might be.

—Lakshmi Mittal

An idea can turn to dust or magic, depending on the talent that rubs against it.

—Bill Bernbach

**Be realistic. Plan for a miracle.**

—Bhagwan Shree Rajneesh

Character is doing the right thing when nobody's looking.

—J.C. Watts

Even if you're on the right track, you'll get run over if you just sit there.

—Will Rogers

Do all the good you can, and make as little fuss about it as possible.

—Charles Dickens

 # Inspirational

Don't wait for your ship to come in— swim out to it.

—Author Unknown

—Author Unknown

**Flexible people don't get bent out of shape.**

Excellence is doing our best, and that's achievable. Perfection isn't.

—Rita Emmett

Discovery consists of looking at the same thing as everyone else does and thinking something different.

—Albert Szent-Gyorgyi

Do not look to the ground for your next step; greatness lies with those who look to the horizon.

—Norwegian Proverb

*Do something every day for no other reason than you would rather not do it, so that when the hour of dire need draws nigh, it may find you not unnerved and untrained to stand the test.*

—William James

Dreams are renewable. No matter what our age or condition, there are still untapped possibilities within us and new beauty waiting to be born.

—Dale Turner

Face new challenges, seize new opportunities, test your resources against the unknown and in the process, discover your own unique potential.

—John Amatt

Fear less, hope more; eat less, chew more; whine less, breathe more; talk less, say more; hate less, love more; and all good things are yours.

—Swedish Proverb

Follow your instincts. That's where true wisdom manifests itself.

—Oprah Winfrey

I'm not telling you it is going to be easy— I'm telling you it's going to be worth it.

—Art Williams

I am not a has-been. I am a will be.

—Lauren Bacall

If nothing ever changed, there'd be no butterflies.

—Author Unknown

# Inspirational

**Imagine.**

*Inspire:*
*To motivate one to action.*

If you are dissatisfied with the way things are, then YOU have got to resolve to change them.
—Barbara Jordan

In order to succeed, your desire for success should be greater than your fear of failure.
—Bill Cosby

Remember, Ginger Rogers did everything Fred Astaire did, but backwards and in high heels.
—Faith Whittlesey

Happiness is not a destination. It is a method of life.
—Burton Hills

Hold yourself responsible for a higher standard than anyone else expects of you. Never excuse yourself.
—Henry Ward Beecher

If we did all the things that we are capable of doing, we would literally astound ourselves.
—Thomas Edison

It does not do to dwell on dreams and forget to live, remember that.

—J.K. Rowling, *Harry Potter and The Sorcerer's Stone*

It is not the strongest of the species that survive, nor the most intelligent, but the one most responsive to change.

—Author Unknown

It is up to you to illuminate the world.

—Phillippe Venier

It takes a great deal of bravery to stand up to our enemies, just as much to stand up to our friends.

—J.K. Rowling, *Harry Potter and The Sorcerer's Stone*

Keep your fears to yourself, but share your courage with others.

—Robert Louis Stevenson

Keep your face to the sunshine and you cannot see the shadow.

—Helen Keller

Learn all you can from the mistakes of others. You won't have time to make them all yourself.

—Alfred Sheinwold

It's what you learn after you know it all that counts.

—John Wooden

# Inspirational

## Live in the sunshine, swim the sea, drink the wild air.

—Ralph Waldo Emerson

Life is short, break the rules, forgive quickly, kiss slowly, love truly, laugh uncontrollably, and never regret anything that made you smile.

Let me tell you the secret that has led me to my goal: My strength lies solely in my tenacity.

—Louis Pasteur

Let us remember that, as much has been given us, much will be expected from us, and that true homage comes from the heart as well as from the lips, and shows itself in deeds.

—Theodore Roosevelt

*Life involves passions, faiths, doubts and courage.*

—Josiah Royce

Life is like riding a bicycle.
To keep your balance, you must keep moving.

—Albert Einstein

*Life is not a matter of holding good cards, but sometimes, playing a poor hand well.*

—Jack London

Move out of your comfort zone. You can only grow if you are willing to feel awkward and uncomfortable when you try something new.

—Brian Tracy

No matter what anybody tells you, words and ideas can change the world.

—Robin Williams, *Dead Poet's Society*

Nothing in life is to be feared. It is only to be understood.

—Marie Curie

In matters of style, swim with the current; in matters of principle, stand like a rock.

—Thomas Jefferson

*Our lives improve only when we take chances— and the first and most difficult risk we can take is to be honest with ourselves.*

—Walter Anderson

Pick battles big enough to matter, small enough to win.

—Jonathan Kozel

**Plant your feet firmly and let your heart have wings.**

# Inspirational

The man who is swimming against the stream knows the strength of it.

—Woodrow T. Wilson

Success means we go to sleep at night knowing that our talents and abilities were used in a way that served others.

—Marianne Williamson

The odds of hitting your target go up dramatically when you aim at it.

—Mal Pancoast

The best way to predict the future is to invent it.

—Alan Kay

Perseverance is a great element of success. If you only knock long enough and loud enough at the gate, you are sure to wake up somebody.

—Henry Wadsworth Longfellow

Sometimes your only available transportation is a leap of faith.

—Margaret Shepard

There are generations yet unborn, whose very lives will be shifted and shaped by the moves you make and the actions you take.

—Andy Andrews

The best executive is the one who has sense enough to pick good men to do what he wants done, and self-restraint enough to keep from meddling with them while they do it.

—Theodore Roosevelt

The block of granite which was an obstacle in the pathway of the weak, becomes a stepping-stone in the pathway of the strong.

—Thomas Carlyle

*The golden opportunity you are seeking is in yourself. It is not in your environment; it is not in luck or chance, or the help of others; it is in yourself alone.*

—Orison Swett Marden

# The past does not define you, the present does.

—Jillian Michaels

*The world needs dreamers and the world needs doers. But above all, the world needs dreamers who do.*

—Sarah Ban Breathnach

The way to succeed is to double your error rate.

—Thomas J. Watson

*There is no try. There is either do or do not.*

—Yoda

# Laughter

You're never too old
to do GOoFY stuff.

~Ward Cleaver

A celebrity is a person who works hard all his life to become well-known, then wears dark glasses to avoid being recognized.

—Fred Allen

A consultant is someone who takes a subject you understand and makes it sound confusing.

*A laugh is a smile that bursts.*

—Mary H. Waldrip

*A synonym is a word you use when you can't spell the word you first thought of.*

—Burt Bacharach

All my life I've wanted, just once, to say something clever without losing my train of thought.

—Robert Brault

Anyone who lives within their means suffers from a lack of imagination.

—Oscar Wilde

Always remember that you are absolutely unique. Just like everyone else.

Before you criticize someone, you should walk a mile in their shoes. That way, when you criticize them, you're a mile away and you have their shoes.

—Author Unknown

# Laughter

I don't mind going back to daylight saving time. With inflation, the hour will be the only thing I've saved all year.

—Victor Borge

*I am thankful for laughter, except when milk comes out of my nose.*

—Woody Allen

I bought some batteries, but they weren't included.

—Steven Wright

I cook with wine, sometimes I even add it to the food.

—W. C. Fields

Don't worry about the world coming to an end today. It is already tomorrow in Australia.

—Charles Schulz

Duct tape is like the force. It has a light side, a dark side, and it holds the universe together.

—Carl Zwanzig

Everyone has a photographic memory. Some just don't have film.

Few things are more satisfying than seeing your children have teenagers of their own.

—Doug Larson

I used to have an open mind but my brains kept falling out.

I like my money right where I can see it: hanging in my closet.

—From the television show *Sex and the City*

I used to eat a lot of natural foods until I learned that most people die of natural causes.

—Author Unknown

*If life is a bowl of cherries, why am I stuck with the pits?*

If people concentrated on the really important things in life, there'd be a shortage of fishing poles.

—Doug Larson

If people were meant to pop out of bed, we'd all sleep in toasters.

—Author Unknown

**If you can't convince them, confuse them.**

—Harry S. Truman

*If you can't be kind, at least have the decency to be vague.*

—Jerry Seinfeld

# Laughter

**Laughter is an instant vacation.**

—Milton Berle

*Never have more children than you have car windows.*

—Erma Bombeck

*Laughter gives us distance.*
*It allows us to step back from an event,*
*deal with it and then move on.*

—Bob Newhart

If you think nobody cares if you're alive, try missing a couple of car payments.

—Earl Wilson

*It is amazing how quickly the kids learn to drive a car, yet a re unable to understand the lawnmower, snowblower or vacuum cleaner.*

—Ben Bergor

It would seem that something which means poverty, disorder and violence every single day should be avoided entirely, but the desire to beget children is a natural urge.

—Phyllis Diller

Never lend your car to anyone to whom you have given birth.

—Erma Bombeck

Older people shouldn't eat health food, they need all the preservatives they can get.

—Robert Orben

People are living longer than ever before, a phenomenon undoubtedly made necessary by the 30-year mortgage.

—Doug Larson

Procrastination is the art of keeping up with yesterday.

—Don Marquis

## Remember, men need laughter sometimes more than food.

—Anna Fellows Johnston

The best substitute for experience is being 16.

—Raymond Duncan

The best measure of a man's honesty isn't his income tax return. It's the zero adjust on his bathroom scale.

—Arthur C. Clarke

Love

Love puts the fun in TOGETHER
the sad in APART,
and the joy in a HEART.

*A dream that is dreamed by two is a dream that will come true.*

A good marriage is like a casserole, only those responsible for it really know what goes in it.

—Anonymous

A hundred hearts would be too few, to carry all my love for you.

—Author Unknown

Anniversary: A time to celebrate the beauty, gift and blessing of enduring love.

**Anyone can be passionate, but it takes real lovers to be silly.**

—Rose Franken

Can miles truly separate you from friends ... If you want to be with someone you love, aren't you already there?

—Richard Bach

Being deeply loved by someone gives you strength, while loving someone deeply gives you courage.

—Lao Tzu

*How wonderful the world is because you are in it—hugs and kisses, love and affection.*

**Gravitation is not responsible for people falling in love.**

—Albert Einstein

# Love

Love is a canvas furnished by nature and embroidered by imagination.

—Voltaire

Life has taught us that love does not consist in gazing at each other but in looking outward together in the same direction.

—Antoine de Saint-Exupéry

*I think about you constantly, whether it's with my mind or my heart.*

—Albany Bach Reid

If I had a single flower for every time I think about you, I could walk forever in my garden.

—Claudia Ghandi

If I love you, what business is it of yours?

—Johann Wolfgang von Goethe

*I'm so in love, every time I look at you my soul gets dizzy.*

—Jaesse Tyler

It doesn't matter where you go in life or what you do ... it's who you have beside you.

*Love—a wildly misunderstood although highly desirable malfunction of the heart which weakens the brain, causes eyes to sparkle, cheeks to glow, blood pressure to rise and the lips to pucker.*

—Author Unknown

Love begins at home, and it is not how much we do ... but how much love we put in that action.

—Mother Teresa

*Love begins in a moment, grows over time and lasts for eternity.*

Love is a game that two can play and both win.

—Eva Gabor

Love is an act of endless forgiveness, a tender look which becomes a habit.

—Peter Ustinov

**Love is being stupid together.**

—Paul Valery

Love is a symbol of eternity. It wipes out all sense of time, destroying all memory of a beginning and all fear of an end.

—Author Unknown

Love is the greatest refreshment in life.

—Pablo Picasso

Love is to let those we love be perfectly themselves, and not to twist them to fit our own image ... otherwise we love only the reflection of ourselves we find in them.

—Author Unknown

Love is, above all, the gift of oneself.

—Jean Anouilh

## Love is just a word until someone comes along and gives it meaning.

Love is missing someone whenever you're apart, but somehow feeling warm inside because you're close in heart.

—Kay Knudsen

Love is not blind—
it sees more, not less.
But because it sees more,
it is willing to see less.

—Julius Gordon

Love is the condition in which the happiness of another person is essential to your own.

—Robert Heinlein

*Loving is never a waste of time.*

—Astrid Alauda

Marriage is not a noun; it's a verb.
It isn't something you get. It's something you do.
It's the way you love your partner every day.

—Barbara De Angelis

Married couples who love each other tell each other a thousand things without talking.

—Chinese Proverb

*Sometimes the shortest distance between two points is a winding path walked arm in arm.*

—Robert Brault

## The art of love ... is largely the art of persistence.

—Albert Ellis

*Love of My Life*

Love means nothing in tennis, but it's everything in life.

—Author Unknown

Love's gift cannot be given, it waits to be accepted.

—Rabindranath Tagore

*Love puts the fun in together, the sad in apart and the joy in a heart.*

—Author Unknown

# Milestones

Here's to making dreams come true!

Do not the most moving moments of
our lives find us all without words?

—Marcel Marceau

A graduation ceremony is an event where the commencement
speaker tells thousands of students dressed in identical
caps and gowns that individuality is the key to success.

—Robert Orben

All that stands between the graduate and
the top of the ladder is the ladder.

—Author Unknown

*An investment in knowledge always pays the best interest.*

—Benjamin Franklin

At commencement you wear your
square-shaped mortarboards.
My hope is that from time to time
you will let your minds be bold,
and wear sombreros.

—Paul Freund

*Discover
new
horizons.*

**Every new beginning
comes from some
other beginning's end.**

—Seneca

*Don't live down to
expectations. Go
out there and do
something remarkable.*

—Wendy Wasserstein

## Expect the best!

Gather your dreams.

*I'm proud of you.*

Here's to making dreams come true!

## Hitch your wagon to a star.

—Ralph Waldo Emerson

*Hold on to your dreams.*

I hope your dreams take you to the corners of your smiles, to the highest of your hopes, to the windows of your opportunities and to the most special places your heart has ever known.

—Author Unknown

I think of life as a good book. The further you get into it, the more it begins to make sense.

—Harold S. Kushner

*If you feel that you have both feet planted on level ground, then the university has failed you.*

—Robert Goheen

# If opportunity doesn't knock, build a door.

—Milton Berle

If you take responsibility for yourself you will develop a hunger to accomplish your dreams.

—Les Brown

It takes courage to grow up and become who you really are.

—e.e. cummings

*Learning is like rowing upstream; not to advance is to drop back.*

—Chinese Proverb

Look not mournfully into the past. It comes not back again. Wisely improve the present, it is thine. Go forth to meet the shadowy future, without fear.

—Henry Wadsworth Longfellow

The fireworks begin today. Each diploma is a lighted match, each one of you is a fuse.

—Ed Koch

*Put your future in good hands— your own.*

—Author Unknown

*May your dreams defy the laws of gravity.*

—H. Jackson Brown Jr.

Shoot for the moon. Even if you miss, you'll land among the stars.

—Les Brown

*Wishing you
all the special
joys that life
can bring!*

There will always be dreams grander or humbler than your own, but there will never be a dream exactly like your own … for you are unique and more wondrous than you know!

—Linda Staten

The future depends on what we do in the present.

—Mahatma Gandhi

## The important thing is not to stop questioning.

—Albert Einstein

*The larger the island of knowledge,
the longer the shoreline of wonder.*

—Ralph W. Sockman

The tassel's worth the hassle!

—Author Unknown

There is a good reason they call these ceremonies "commencement exercises."
Graduation is not the end; it's the beginning.

—Orrin Hatch

What lies behind us and what lies before us are tiny matters compared to what lies within us.

—Ralph Waldo Emerson

*Whatever you can do or dream you can do, begin it. Boldness has genius, power and magic in it.*

—Johann Wolfgang von Goethe

You have brains in your head.
You have feet in your shoes.
You can steer yourself in any direction you choose.
You're on your own.
And you know what you know.
You are the guy who'll decide where to go.

—Dr. Seuss, *Oh, The Places You'll Go*

A journey of a thousand miles begins with a single step.

—Lao Tzu

**Your schooling may be over, but remember that your education still continues.**

—Author Unknown

Be well, do good work, and keep in touch.

—Garrison Keillor

*Getting there isn't half the fun, it's all the fun.*

—Robert Townsend

There are no shortcuts to any place worth going.

—Beverly Sills

## Why does it take a minute to say hello and forever to say goodbye?

—Author Unknown

*Wherever you go, go with all your heart!*

—Confucius

Don't be dismayed at goodbyes. A farewell is necessary before you can meet again. And meeting again, after moments or lifetimes, is certain for those who are friends.

—Richard Bach

How lucky I am to have something that makes saying goodbye so hard.

—Carol Sobieski and Thomas Meehan, *Annie*

*It is good to have an end to journey toward, but it is the journey that matters in the end.*

—Ursula K. LeGuin

May you have warm words on a cold evening, a full moon on a dark night and a smooth road all the way to your door.

—Irish Toast

I find the great thing in this world is not so much where we stand, as in what direction we are moving.

—Oliver Wendell Holmes, Jr.

Every house where love abides, and friendship is a guest,
is surely home, and home sweet home,
for there the heart can rest.

—Henry Van Dyke

*God rest his love upon this door and*
*bless this house forevermore.*

It takes hands to build a house,
but only hearts can build a home.

*May good health and happiness herein reside;*
*may the Lord bless this dwelling and all those inside.*

**May love always find the path to your door.**

*May the light of*
*God's love guide*
*your path.*

May love fill your
new home today
and always.

May your new home
be filled with warmth,
laughter and sunshine.

May you have
warmth in
your heart,
peace in
your home.

our life is    something
with the ti    hrough life
g to save    rying to fi

*Whoever is happy will make others happy too.* ~Anne Frank

A cat can be trusted to purr when she is pleased, which is more than can be said for human beings.

—William Ralph Inge

After scolding one's cat, one looks into its face and is seized by the ugly suspicion that it understood every word. And has filed it for reference.

—Charlotte Gray

Cats are intended to teach us that not everything in nature has a purpose.

—Garrison Keillor

# Cats are smarter than dogs. You can't get eight cats to pull a sled through snow.

—Jeff Valdez

Cats can work out mathematically the exact place to sit that will cause most inconvenience.

—Pam Brown

*Happiness is a warm puppy.*

—Charles M. Schulz

Dogs eat. Cats dine.

—Ann Taylor

Have a purr-fect day!

Dogs believe they are human. Cats believe they are God.

—Author Unknown

# Miscellaneous

**If dogs could talk, it would take a lot of the fun out of owning one.**

—Andy Rooney

*A man who carries a cat by the tail learns something he can learn in no other way.*

—Mark Twain

Our perfect companions never have fewer than four feet.

—Colette

Did you ever notice when you blow in a dog's face he gets mad at you? But when you take him in a car, he sticks his head out the window.

—Steve Bluestone

I think dogs are the most amazing creatures; they give unconditional love. For me they are the role model for being alive.

—Gilda Radner

*If animals could speak, the dog would be a blundering outspoken fellow; but the cat would have the rare grace of never saying a word too much.*

—Mark Twain

Just because an animal is large, it doesn't mean he doesn't want kindness; however big Tigger seems to be, remember that he wants as much kindness as Roo.

—Winnie the Pooh (A.A. Milne)

Properly trained, a man can be dog's best friend.

—Corey Ford

Scratch a dog and you'll find a permanent job.

—Franklin P. Jones

*The best way to get a puppy is to beg for a baby brother—and they'll settle for a puppy every time.*

—Winston Pendleton

The cat could very well be man's best friend, but would never stoop to admitting it.

—Doug Larson

**The pug is living proof that God has a sense of humor.**

—Margo Kaufman

*There is something about the presence of a cat ... that seems to take the bite out of being alone.*

—Louis J. Camuti

*The ideal of calm exists in a sitting cat.*

—Jules Renard

**There is no more intrepid explorer than a kitten.**

—Jules Champfleury

There is no psychiatrist in the world like a puppy licking your face.

—Bern Williams

There is, incidentally, no way of talking about cats that enables one to come off as a sane person.

—Dan Greenberg

You can keep a dog; but it is the cat who keeps people, because cats find humans useful domestic animals.

—George Mikes

## What greater gift than the love of a cat?

—Charles Dickens

*Everything I know I learned from my cat:*
*When you're hungry, eat.*
*When you're tired, nap in a sunbeam.*
*When you go to the vet's, pee on your owner.*

—Gary Smith

A good teacher is like a candle—
it consumes itself to light the way for others.

—Author Unknown

## A teacher affects eternity; he can never tell where his influence stops.

—Henry Brooks Adams

*A wise teacher makes learning a joy.*

—Proverb

*Nurses dispense comfort, compassion and caring without even a prescription.*

—Val Saintsbury

Teaching is the profession that teaches all the other professions.

—Author Unknown

Teaching should be full of ideas instead of stuffed with facts.

—Author Unknown

*The art of teaching is the art of assisting discovery.*

—Mark Van Doren

The best teachers teach from the heart, not from the book.

—Author Unknown

**Volunteers are love in motion!**

—Author Unknown

Those who can, do.
Those who can do more, volunteer.

—Author Unknown

What the teacher is, is more important than what he teaches.

—Karl Menninger

Time spent teaching is never lost.

—Native American Proverb

# Miscellaneous

**Leaders don't create followers, they create more leaders.**

—Tom Peters

*A leader is a dealer in hope.*

—Napoleon Bonaparte, attributed

A leader leads by example not by force.

—Sun Tzu

In teaching you cannot see the fruit of a day's work. It is invisible and remains so, maybe for 20 years.

—Jacques Barzun

The mediocre teacher tells.
The good teacher explains.
The superior teacher demonstrates.
The great teacher inspires.

—William Arthur Ward

*When you're a nurse you know that every day you will touch a life or a life will touch yours.*

—Author Unknown

You can teach a student a lesson for a day; but if you can teach him to learn by creating curiosity, he will continue the learning process as long as he lives.

—Clay P. Bedford

*Everyone smiles in the same language.*

—Author Unknown

Half our life is spent trying to find something to do with the time we have rushed through life trying to save.

—Will Rogers

I like to see a man proud of the place in which he lives. I like to see a man live so that his place will be proud of him.

—Abraham Lincoln

I owe my success to having listened respectfully to the very best advice, and then going away and doing the exact opposite.

—G.K. Chesterton

*Rivers know this: There is no hurry. We shall get there some day.*

—Winnie the Pooh (A.A. Milne)

If you don't think every day is a good day, just try missing one.

—Cavett Robert

**Whoever is happy will make others happy too.**

—Anne Frank

# Parenting

A mother is always close to your heart, whether near in miles or far apart.

*A grandfather is someone with silver in his hair and gold in his heart.*

—Author Unknown

A grandparent is old on the outside but young on the inside.

—Author Unknown

A house needs a grandma in it.

—Louisa May Alcott

A mother is a person who, seeing there are only four pieces of pie for five people, promptly announces she never did care for pie.

—Tenneva Jordan

A mother is always close to your heart, whether near in miles or far apart.

Being grandparents sufficiently removes us from the responsibilities so that we can be friends.

—Allan Frome

*Any mother could perform the jobs of several air traffic controllers with ease.*

—Lisa Alther

**Dad, your guiding hand on my shoulder will remain with me forever.**

—Author Unknown

Children aren't happy with nothing to ignore, and that's what parents were created for.

—Ogden Nash

# Parenting

## Grandmas never run out of hugs or cookies.

—Author Unknown

*Grandmother-grandchild relationships are simple. Grandmas are short on criticism and long on love.*

—Author Unknown

Grandmothers are special.

*Grandpas are great.*

## Father knows best.

Fatherhood is pretending the present you love most is soap-on-a-rope.

—Bill Cosby

Few things are more delightful than grandchildren fighting over your lap.

—Doug Larson

Grandfathers are for loving and fixing things.

—Author Unknown

*Grandma always made you feel she had been waiting to see just you all day and now the day was complete.*

—Marcy DeMaree

Grandparents are similar to a piece of string—handy to have around and easily wrapped around the fingers of their grandchildren.

—Author Unknown

*He didn't tell me how to live; he lived, and let me watch him do it.*

—Clarence Budington Kelland

I love my mother as the trees love water and sunshine—she helps me grow, prosper and reach great heights.

—Terri Guillemets

If nothing is going well, call your grandmother.

—Italian Proverb

Mother—that was the bank where we deposited all our hurts and worries.

—T. DeWitt Talmage

**Mother's love grows by giving.**

—Charles Lamb

The best place to be when you're sad is Grandpa's lap.

—Author Unknown

*My grandkids believe I'm the oldest thing in the world. And after two or three hours with them, I believe it too.*

—Gene Perret

Parenting

One of the most powerful handclasps is that of a new grandbaby around the finger of a grandfather.

—Joy Hargrove

The mother's heart is the child's schoolroom.

—Henry Ward Beecher

*The phrase "working mother" is redundant.*

—Jane Sellman

There's nothing like a mama-hug.

—Adabella Radici

It's not only children who grow.  Parents do too. As much as we watch to see what our children do with their lives, they are watching us to see what we do with ours. I can't tell my children to reach for the sun. All I can do is reach for it myself.

—Joyce Maynard

Most of all the other beautiful things in life come by twos and threes, by dozens and hundreds.  Plenty of roses, stars, sunsets, rainbows, brothers and sisters, aunts and cousins, comrades and friends— but only one mother in the whole world.

—Kate Douglas Wiggin

My father used to play with my brother and me in the yard. Mother would come out and say, "You're tearing up the grass." "We're not raising grass," Dad would reply. "We're raising boys."

—Harmon Killebrew

My mom is a never-ending song in my heart of comfort, happiness and being. I may sometimes forget the words but I always remember the tune.

—Graycie Harmon

*The best conversations with mothers always take place in silence, when only the heart speaks.*

—Carrie Latet

*When you are a mother, you are never really alone in your thoughts. A mother always has to think twice, once for herself and once for her child.*

—Sophia Loren

**There are two lasting bequests we can give our children: one is roots, the other is wings.**

—Hodding Carter, Jr.

The tie which links mother and child is of such pure and immaculate strength as to be never violated.

—Washington Irving

# Religious

Today is God's gift
to you ...
Each day you are God's gift
to me!

HAPPY BIRTHDAY

All I have seen teaches me to trust the Creator for all I have not seen.

—Ralph Waldo Emerson

Art is a reflection of God's creativity, an evidence that we are made in the image of God.

—Francis Schaeffer

As for me and my house, we will serve the Lord.

—Joshua 24:15 (New American Standard Bible)

Be still and know that I am God.

—Psalm 46:10 (New International Version)

Behold, I show you a mystery; we shall not all sleep, but we shall all be changed, in a moment, in the twinkling of an eye.

—I Corinthians 15:51-52 (King James Version)

Come near to God, and He will come near to you.

—James 4:8 (New International Version)

Courage is contagious. When a brave man takes a stand, the spines of others are often stiffened.

—Billy Graham

Doubt springs from the mind. Faith is the daughter of the soul.

—J. Pete Senn

# Religious

God is our refuge and strength, a very present help in trouble.

—Psalm 46:1 (King James Version)

## God enters by a private door into every individual.

—Ralph Waldo Emerson

*God never shuts one door but He opens another.*

—Irish Proverb

God gives us dreams a size too big so that we can grow in them.

—Author Unknown

Everything comes from God alone. Everything lives by His power, and everything is for His glory.

—Romans 11:36 (The Living Bible)

Everything on earth has its own time and its own season.

—Ecclesiastes 3:1 (Contemporary English Version)

*Faith is the strength by which a shattered world shall emerge into the light.*

—Helen Keller

*Faith leads us beyond ourselves. It leads us directly to God.*

—Pope John Paul II

Faith sees the invisible, believes the unbelievable and receives the impossible.

—Corrie Ten Boom

God's heart is the most sensitive and tender of all.
No act goes unnoticed, no matter how insignificant or small.

—Richard J. Foster

## Grace and peace be yours in abundance.

—2 Peter 1:2 (New International Version)

Great opportunities often
disguise themselves in small tasks.

—Rick Warren

He is no fool who gives what he cannot
keep to gain what he cannot lose.

—Jim Elliot

Their wings wrap gently around you,
whispering you are loved and blessed.

—Angel Blessing

I am your Creator.
You were in my care even
before you were born.

—Isaiah 44:2 (Contemporary English Version)

*I know that my
Redeemer liveth.*

—Job 19:25 (American Standard Version)

*History belongs to the
intercessors—those
who believe and pray
the future into being.*

—Walter Wink

Humility is not thinking
less of yourself; it's
thinking of yourself less.

—Rick Warren

# Religious

Living for God's glory is the greatest achievement we can accomplish with our lives.

—Rick Warren

Lift up your eyes.
The heavenly Father waits to bless you—
in inconceivable ways to make your life what you never dreamed it could be.

—Anne Ortlund

**If God can work through me, He can work through anyone.**

—St. Francis of Assisi

If I have enjoyed the hospitality of the Host of this universe, who daily spreads a table in my sight, surely I cannot do less than acknowledge my dependence.

—G.A. Johnston Ross

If we only have the will to walk,
then God is pleased with our stumbles.

—C.S. Lewis

*It is God himself who has made us what we are and given us new lives from Christ Jesus; and long ages ago He planned that we should spend these lives in helping others.*

—Ephesians 2:10 (The Living Bible)

It is the fire of suffering that brings forth the gold of godliness.

—Madame Guyon

Let your roots grow down into Christ and draw up nourishment from Him. See that you go on growing in the Lord, and become strong and vigorous in the truth.

—Colossians 2:7 (The Living Bible)

Lord, remind me how brief my time on earth will be. Remind me that my days are numbered— how fleeting my life is.

—Psalm 39:4 (New Living Translation)

*Lord, when we are wrong, make us willing to change; where we are right, make us easy to live with.*

—Peter Marshall

*Love the Lord your God with all your heart and with all your soul and with all your mind and with all your strength.*

—Mark 12:30 (New International Version)

**Never think that God's delays are God's denials. Hold on; hold fast; hold out. Patience is genius.**

—Georges-Louis Leclerc de Buffon

May the promise of God's Word be your hope today, your peace tomorrow and your comfort always.

#  Religious

**Reverence invites Revelation**

*See how very much our heavenly Father loves us, for He allows us to be called His children, and we really are!*

—I John 3:1 (New Living Translation)

Many are the plans in a man's heart, but it is the Lord's purpose that prevails.

—Proverbs 19:21 (New International Version)

She who kneels before God, can stand before anyone.

The fewer the words, the better the prayer.

—Martin Luther

*No one who meets Jesus ever stays the same.*

—Philip Yancey

One should not stand at the foot of a sick person's bed, because that place is reserved for the guardian angel.

—Jewish Folk Saying

Our life is full of brokenness—broken relationships, broken promises, broken expectations. How can we live with that brokenness without becoming bitter and resentful except by returning again and again to God's faithful presence in our lives.

—Henri Nouwen

Peace cannot be achieved through violence, it can only be attained through understanding.

—Ralph Waldo Emerson

Peace I leave with you, my peace I give unto you: not as the world giveth, give I unto you. Let not your heart be troubled, neither let it be afraid.

—John 14:27 (King James Version)

Smile on me, your servant; teach me the right way to live.

—Psalm 119:135 (The Message)

*Take the first step in faith. You don't have to see the whole staircase, just take the first step.*

—Dr. Martin Luther King, Jr.

There is more hunger in the world for love and appreciation than for bread.

—Mother Teresa

The measure of a Christian is not in the height of his grasp but in the depth of his love.

—Clarence Jordan

We should live our lives as though Christ were coming this afternoon.

—Jimmy Carter

**Today is God's gift to you … each day you are God's gift to me!**

# Seasons

There is a way
that nature speaks

A perfect summer day is when the sun is shining, the breeze is blowing, the birds are singing and the lawn mower is broken.

—James Dent

*April hath put a Spirit of youth in everything.*

—William Shakespeare

April prepares her green traffic light and the world thinks Go.

—Christopher Morley, *John Mistletoe*

*Autumn is a second spring when every leaf is a flower.*

—Albert Camus

Be like the flower, turn your face to the sun.

—Kahlil Gibran

Buttercups and daisies, oh, the pretty flowers; coming ere the springtime, to tell of sunny hours.

—Mary Howitt

Bittersweet October. The mellow, messy, leaf-kicking, perfect pause between the opposing miseries of summer and winter.

—Carol Bishop Hipps

**Deep summer is when laziness finds respectability.**

—Sam Keen

There is a way that nature speaks.

# *Seasons*

**Have a sunshine day.**

In seed time learn,
in harvest teach,
in winter enjoy.

—William Blake

In summer, the
song sings itself.

—William Carlos Williams

*If a June night could talk, it would probably boast it invented romance.*

—Bern Williams

Do what we can, summer will have its flies.

—Ralph Waldo Emerson

Don't ignore the small things
—the kite flies because of its tail.

—Hawaiian Proverb

*Even in winter an isolated patch of
snow has a special quality.*

—Andy Goldsworthy

*Everyone must take time to sit
and watch the leaves turn.*

—Elizabeth Lawrence

For man, autumn is a time of harvest, of gathering together.
For nature, it is a time of sowing, of scattering abroad.

—Edwin Way Teale

In the spring, at the end of the day, you should smell like dirt.

—Margaret Atwood

Is it so small a thing, to have enjoyed the sun,
to have lived light in the spring,
to have loved, to have thought, to have done?

—Matthew Arnold

*It was one of those perfect English autumnal days
which occur more frequently in memory than in life.*

—P. D. James

Knowing trees, I understand the meaning of patience.
Knowing grass, I can appreciate persistence.

—Hal Borland

*Live each season as it passes; breath the air,
drink the drink, taste the fruit and resign
yourself to the influences of each.*

—Henry David Thoreau

No spring nor summer
beauty hath such grace
as I have seen in one
autumnal face.

—John Donne

*O, wind, if winter
comes, can spring
be far behind?*

—Percy Bysshe Shelley

October is a symphony of
permanence and change.

—Bonaro W. Overstreet

Nature always has
something rare to show us.

—John Muir, *The Mountains of California*

Spring unlocks the flowers to paint the laughing soil.

—Bishop Reginald Heber

*Spring is when you feel like whistling even with a shoe full of slush.*

—Doug Larson

Spring makes its own statement, so loud and clear that the gardener seems to be only one of the instruments, not the composer.

—Geoffrey B. Charlesworth

Spring shows what God can do with a drab and dirty world.

—Virgil A. Kraft

October's poplars are flaming torches lighting the way to winter.

—Nova Bair

*People don't notice whether it's winter or summer when they're happy.*

—Anton Chekhov

Spring comes: The flowers learn their colored shapes.

—Maria Konopnicka

*Spring has sprung!*

**Soak up the sun.**

*Summer love, midnight kisses, shooting stars, secret wishes.*

Summer's filled with breaking the rules, standing apart, ignoring your head and following your heart.

—Author Unknown

*Sun is shining, the weather is sweet. Make you wanna move your dancing feet.*

—Bob Marley, *Sun is Shining*

## The best thing one can do when it's raining is to let it rain.

—Henry Wadsworth Longfellow

The color of springtime is in the flowers, the color of winter is in the imagination.

—Terri Guillemets

The seasons are what a symphony ought to be: Four perfect movements in harmony with each other.

—Arthur Rubenstein

The leaves fall, the wind blows and the farm country slowly changes from the summer cottons into its winter wools.

—Henry Beston

The tans will fade, but the memories will last forever.

# Sympathy

Our hearts, our prayers, and our love are with you.

A heartfelt message in this hour of sorrow:
May you find new courage for each new tomorrow.

—Author Unknown

*Although it's difficult today to see
beyond the sorrow, may looking back
in memory help comfort you tomorrow.*

—Author Unknown

*As you comprehend this profound loss,
let yourself cry knowing each tear is a
note of love rising to the heavens.*

—Author Unknown

Although we know at such a time
there's little we can say,
we want to let you know that
you're in our thoughts today.

—Author Unknown

Find comfort, strength
and peace knowing
others care, because you
are remembered in every
thought and prayer.

—Author Unknown

Hearts can feel so
many things words
cannot convey, such as
the loving sympathy
felt for you today.

—Author Unknown

# Sympathy

*If the future seems overwhelming, remember that it comes one moment at a time.*

—Beth Mende Conny

In the night
of death,
hope sees a star,
and listening love
can hear the
rustle of a wing.

—Robert Green Ingersoll

Like a bird singing in the rain, let grateful memories survive in time of sorrow.

—Robert Louis Stevenson

Be comforted at this most difficult time knowing that you are surrounded by many who understand and are nearby to help, for they too share in your sorrow and loss.

Death is not extinguishing the light; it is only putting out the lamp because the dawn has come.

—Rabindranath Tagore

Hold tight to memories for comfort, lean on your friends for strength and always remember how much you are cared about.

—Author Unknown

I know for certain that we never lose the people we love, even to death. They continue to participate in every act, thought and decision we make. Their love leaves an indelible imprint in our memories. We find comfort in knowing that our lives have been enriched by having shared their love.

—Leo Buscaglia

In the stars that shine, the flowers that bloom or in a gentle breeze, may you feel the presence of your loved one and be comforted by treasured memories.

—Author Unknown

*Life is eternal, and love is immortal, and death is only a horizon; and a horizon is nothing save the limit of our sight.*

—Rossiter W. Raymond

*May God's grace strengthen you.*

**May it bring you some comfort to know how many warm and caring thoughts go out to you in your time of sorrow.**

May the blessings of love be upon you. May its peace abide with you. May its essence illuminate your heart, now and forever more.

—Sufi Blessing

# Sympathy

*Our hearts go out to you in your time of sorrow.*

Our loving thoughts and prayers are with you and your entire family.

*Remember that we love and care about you.*

Our hearts, our prayers and our love are with you.

May the sorrow that you're feeling now eventually give way, as cherished memories give you the strength to face each future day.

—Author Unknown

*May you have memories to turn to for comfort, friends to turn to for support and faith in God to give you hope, strength and courage.*

May you take comfort in knowing an angel is watching over you.

Oh heart, if one should say to you that the soul perishes like the body, answer that the flower withers, but the seed remains.

—Kahlil Gibran

*Our hearts are filled with sorrow.*

*Please accept our most heartfelt sympathies for your loss … our thoughts are with you and your family during this difficult time.*

Though nothing can bring back the hour of splendor in the grass, glory in the flower, we will grieve not, rather find strength in what remains behind.

—William Wordsworth

Times of loss and sorrow must come to all who live. And though the words of comfort are difficult to give, still perhaps you'll understand what words can never say. And know the heartfelt sympathy that comes to you today.

—Author Unknown

*When someone you love becomes a memory, the memory becomes a treasure.*

—Author Unknown

**To live in hearts we leave behind is not to die.**

—Thomas Campbell, *Hallowed Ground*

**With thoughts of peace and courage for you.**

We are deeply saddened by your loss. We will cherish the memories of the times we spent together. We are with you during this time of grief.

# Thank You

Thanks . . . not just for the BIG things you do, but all the **wonderful** *little* things too!

A fellow who does things that count,
doesn't usually stop to count them.

—Author Unknown

## A hug is a great gift—one size fits all, and it's easy to exchange.

—Author Unknown

A thankful heart is not only the greatest virtue,
but the parent of all the other virtues.

—Cicero

*Accept my endless gratitude.*

*As much as we need a prosperous economy,
we also need a prosperity of kindness and decency.*

—Caroline Kennedy

Compassion brings us to
a stop, and for a moment
we rise above ourselves.

—Mason Cooley

Blessed are those who can
give without remembering
and take without forgetting.

—Elizabeth Bibesco

*Feeling gratitude and
not expressing it is like
wrapping a present
and not giving it.*

—William Arthur Ward

Every time we remember
to say "thank you," we
experience nothing less
than heaven on earth.

—Sara Ban Breathnach

# Thank You

*I am overwhelmed with gratitude.*

I awoke this morning with devout thanksgiving for my friends, the old and the new.

—Ralph Waldo Emerson

Gratitude unlocks the fullness of life... It can turn a meal into a feast, a house into a home, a stranger into a friend. Gratitude makes sense of our past, brings peace for today and creates a vision for tomorrow.

—Melody Beattie

For your thoughtfulness and generosity, from you I have learned much of life's philosophy. Thank you sincerely.

—Author Unknown

Give thanks for a little and you will find a lot.

—The Hausa of Nigeria

**Gratitude is the best attitude.**

—Author Unknown

*There is not a more pleasing exercise of the mind than gratitude. It is accompanied with such an inward satisfaction that the duty is sufficiently rewarded by the performance.*

—Joseph Addison

I expect to pass through this world but once; any good thing therefore that I can do, or any kindness that I can show to any fellow creature, let me do it now; let me not defer or neglect it, for I shall not pass this way again.

—Stephen Grellet

I feel a very unusual sensation—if it is not indigestion, I think it must be gratitude.

—Benjamin Disraeli

I find that the more willing I am to be grateful for the small things in life, the bigger stuff just seems to show up from unexpected sources, and I am constantly looking forward to each day with all the surprises that keep coming my way!

—Louise L. Hay

If you want others to be happy, practice compassion. If you want to be happy, practice compassion.

—Dalai Lama

I would maintain that thanks are the highest form of thought, and that gratitude is happiness doubled by wonder.

—G.K. Chesterton

Just a "thank you" is a mighty powerful prayer. Says it all.

—Rosie Cash

Joyfulness keeps the heart and face young. A good laugh makes us better friends with ourselves and everybody around us.

—Orison Swett Marden

# Thank You

*Thank you for never letting me down.*

Thanks for being my friend. Thanks for thinking about me. Thanks for caring about me. Thanks for everything you did for me. You shouldn't have, but I'm so glad you did.

—Author Unknown

Kindness, like a boomerang, always returns.

—Author Unknown

Let us be grateful to people who make us happy; they are the charming gardeners who make our souls blossom.

—Marcel Proust

*Life becomes harder for us when we live for others, but it also becomes richer and happier.*

—Albert Schweitzer

Of all the "attitudes" we can acquire, surely the attitude of gratitude is the most important and by far the most life-changing.

—Zig Ziglar

## Sometimes the best helping hand you can give is a good, firm push.

—Joann Thomas

*Thanks—not just for the big things you do, but all the wonderful little things too!*

The best portion of a good man's life is his little, nameless, unremembered acts of kindness and of love.

—William Wordsworth

## The little things? The little moments? They aren't little.

—Jon Kabat-Zinn

The value of a man resides in what he gives and not in what he is capable of receiving.

—Albert Einstein

There is always, always, always something to be thankful for.

—Author Unknown

Treat people as if they were what they ought to be and you help them to become what they are capable of being.

—Johann Wolfgang von Goethe

*Those who bring sunshine into the lives of others cannot keep it from themselves*

—J. M. Barrie

# Words of Wisdom

Beginnings are scary.

Endings are usually sad,

But it's the middle that counts the most

A man can't make a place for himself in the sun if he keeps taking refuge under the family tree.

—Helen Keller

**A man who limits his interests, limits his life.**

—Vincent Price

Always watch where you are going. Otherwise, you may step on a piece of the forest that was left out by mistake.

—Winnie the Pooh (A.A. Milne)

Art washes away from the soul the dust of everyday life.

—Pablo Picasso

*As I grow older, I pay less attention to what men say. I just watch what they do.*

—Andrew Carnegie

Bad habits are like a comfortable bed, easy to get into, but hard to get out of.

—Author Unknown

Balance, peace and joy are the fruit of a successful life. It starts with recognizing your talents and finding ways to serve others by using them.

—Thomas Kinkade

*Associate yourself with men of good quality if you esteem your own reputation; for 'tis better to be alone than in bad company.*

—George Washington

# Words of Wisdom

*Experience is a comb which nature gives us when we are bald.*

—Belgian Proverb

**Eating words has never given me indigestion.**

—Winston Churchill

Be thankful for what you have and you will end up having more. But if you concentrate on what you don't have, you will never, ever have enough.

—Oprah Winfrey

Being happy doesn't mean that everything is perfect. It means that you've decided to look beyond the imperfections.

—Author Unknown

*Change always comes bearing gifts.*

—Price Pritchett

Criticism is something we can avoid easily by saying nothing, doing nothing and being nothing.

—Aristotle

*Don't worry about people stealing your ideas. If your ideas are any good, you'll have to ram them down people's throats.*

—Howard Aiken

Experience is a hard teacher because she gives the test first, the lesson afterwards.

—Vernon Saunders Law

Experience is not what happens to a man. It is what a man does with what happens to him.

—Aldous Leonard Huxley

# First we make our habits, then our habits make us.

—Author Unknown

*Give to every other human being every right that you claim for yourself.*

—Robert Ingersoll

Good advice is something a man gives when he is too old to set a bad example.

—François de La Rochefoucauld

Happiness comes of the capacity to feel deeply, to enjoy simply, to think freely, to risk life, to be needed.

—Storm Jameson

*Habits are at first cobwebs, then cables.*

—Spanish Proverb

Happiness cannot be traveled to, owned, earned, worn or consumed. Happiness is the spiritual experience of living every minute with love, grace and gratitude.

—Denis Waitley

# Words of Wisdom

If time be of all things most precious, wasting time must be the greatest prodigality; since … lost time is never found again; and what we call time enough always proves little enough.

—Benjamin Franklin

*I would rather regret the things that I have done than the things that I have not.*

—Lucille Ball

*If you don't create change, change will create you.*

—Author Unknown

Happiness is as a butterfly which, when pursued, is always beyond our grasp, but which if you will sit down quietly, may alight upon you.

—Nathaniel Hawthorne

He who has done his best for his own time has lived for all times.

—Friedrich Schiller

*Beginnings are scary, Endings are usually sad, But it's the middle that counts the most.*

**I am not young enough to know everything.**

—Oscar Wilde

I don't know the key to success, but the key to failure is trying to please everybody.

—Bill Cosby

*If you judge people,*
*you have no time to love them.*

—Mother Teresa

If you want children to keep their feet on the ground,
put some responsibility on their shoulders.

—Abigail Van Buren

It's all right letting yourself go,
as long as you can get yourself back.

—Mick Jagger

*It's not enough to be busy ... the question is:*
*What are we busy about?*

—Henry David Thoreau

Language is the dress of thought;
every time you talk your mind is on parade.

—Author Unknown

**Never be in a hurry; do everything quietly and in a calm spirit. Do not lose your inner peace for anything whatsoever, even if your whole world seems upset.**

—St. Francis de Sales

Men are like steel.
When they lose their temper,
they lose their worth.

—Chuck Norris

Never look down
on anybody
unless you're
helping him up.

—Jesse Jackson

# Words of Wisdom

**People who fight fire with fire usually end up with ashes.**

—Abigail Van Buren

One's first step in wisdom is to question everything—and one's last is to come to terms with everything.

—Georg Christoph Lichtenberg

*Peace begins with a smile.*

—Mother Teresa

Ninety-nine percent of the failures come from people who have the habit of making excuses.

—George Washington Carver

No one can make you feel inferior without your consent.

—Eleanor Roosevelt

*"Old times" never come back and I suppose it's just as well. What comes back is a new morning every day in the year, and that's better.*

—George Edward Woodberry

Once the game is over, the king and the pawn go back in the same box.

—Italian Proverb

One of the nice things about problems is that a good many of them do not exist except in our imaginations.

—Steve Allen

# Practice isn't the thing you do once you're good. It's the thing you do that makes you good.

—Malcolm Gladwell

Remember, people will judge you by your actions, not your intentions. You may have a heart of gold— but so does a hard-boiled egg.

—Author Unknown

Self-pity is our worst enemy and if we yield to it, we can never do anything wise in this world.

—Helen Keller

Simplicity is the ultimate sophistication.

—Leonardo da Vinci

*So many fail because they don't get started—they don't go. They don't overcome inertia. They don't begin.*

—W. Clement Stone

Take a music bath once or twice a week for a few seasons, and you will find that it is to the soul what the water bath is to the body.

—Oliver Wendell Holmes

Sometimes when you sacrifice something precious, you're not really losing it. You're just passing it on to someone else.

—Mitch Albom, *The Five People You Meet in Heaven*

# Words of Wisdom

## The less routine the more life.

—Amos Bronson Alcott

The greater our knowledge increases, the greater our ignorance unfolds.

—John F. Kennedy

Tension is who you think you should be. Relaxation is who you are.

—Chinese Proverb

*That you may retain your self-respect, it is better to displease the people by doing what you know is right, than to temporarily please them by doing what you know is wrong.*

—William J.H. Boetcker

The act of putting pen to paper encourages pause for thought, this in turn makes us think more deeply about life, which helps us regain our equilibrium.

—Norbet Platt

*The best cure for worry, depression, melancholy, brooding, is to go deliberately forth and try to lift with one's sympathy the gloom of somebody else.*

—Arnold Bennett

The life of every man is a diary in which he means to write one story, and writes another.

—J. M. Barrie

The measure of a man's real character is what he would do if he knew he would never be found out.

—Thomas Babington Macaulay

The one who asks questions doesn't lose his way.

—African Proverb

The praise that comes from love does not make us vain, but more humble.

—J. M. Barrie

# The purpose of life is a life of purpose.

—Robert Byrne

The time for action is now. It's never too late to do something.

—Antoine de Saint-Exupery

The recipe for perpetual ignorance is: Be satisfied with your opinions and content with your knowledge.

—Elbert Hubbard

There can be no happiness if the things we believe in are different from the things we do.

—Freya Madeline Stark

The time to relax is when you don't have time for it.

—Sidney J. Harris

# My Favorite Quotes

# My Favorite Quotes

_____

_____

_____

_____

_____

_____

_____

_____

_____

_____

_____

_____

## PROJECT CREDITS AND SOURCE LIST

A special thank you goes to Adrienne Kennedy from My Sentiments Exactly! and Elizabeth Gray from Stampin' Up! for providing us with the cards featured on our chapter intro pages. Below is a list of products used to create each of these projects.

**Birthday, pg. 6**
**Sources:** Printed paper from BasicGrey; mirror paper from Worldwin Papers; stamps from MSE!; ribbon from Fancy Pants Designs; silver glitter embellishment from Hobby Lobby Stores Inc.; Design Adhesives circle and glitter from Clearsnap Inc.

**Christmas, pg. 14**
**Sources:** Card stock, dye ink pads, thread, brads and embossing folder from Stampin' Up!; embossing machine from Sizzix.

**Encouragement, pg. 22**
**Sources:** Printed paper from BasicGrey; stamps from MSE!; ribbon from Creative Impressions Inc.; flower from Prima Marketing Inc.; ribbon buckle from Making Memories.

**Family, pg. 32**
**Sources:** Printed paper from Crate Paper Inc.; stamps from MSE!; fine-detail ink pad from Tsukineko LLC; glitter pens from American Crafts Inc.; flowers from Prima Marketing Inc.; pearls from Creative Impressions Inc.; die template from Spellbinders™ Paper Arts.

**Friendship, pg. 42**
**Sources:** Printed paper from Scenic Route Paper Co.; stamps from MSE!; chipboard from BasicGrey; brads from K&Company; silk flower from Prima Marketing Inc.; button from Making Memories; ribbon from Creative Impressions Inc.; Design Adhesives butterflies from Clearsnap Inc.

**Get Well, pg. 48**
**Sources:** Printed paper from BasicGrey; stamps from MSE!; distress ink pad from Ranger Industries Inc.; bird and jewels from Heidi Swapp; paint from Making Memories; flowers from All Natural Accents; ribbon from Fancy Pants Designs.

**Holidays, pg. 54**
**Sources:** Printed paper from BasicGrey; stamps from MSE!; distress ink pad from Ranger Industries Inc.; shimmer spritz from Clearsnap Inc.; flower from K&Company; circle template from The Crafter's Workshop.

**Inspirational, pg. 62**
**Sources:** Printed paper from BasicGrey; stamps from MSE!; fine-detail ink pad from Tsukineko LLC; ribbon from Creative Impressions Inc.; pearls from Hobby Lobby Stores Inc.; Design Adhesives flourish and glitter from Clearsnap Inc.

**Laughter, pg. 72**
**Source:** Card stock, printed paper, ribbon, rhinestones and punches from Stampin' Up!

**Love, pg. 78**
**Sources:** Printed paper from BasicGrey; stamps from MSE!; fine-detail ink pad from Tsukineko LLC; jewels and ribbon from Creative Impressions Inc.; pin from Making Memories; crystal from Hobby Lobby Stores Inc.

**Milestones, pg. 84**
**Sources:** Printed paper from BasicGrey; stamps from MSE!; silver glitter paper from Die Cuts With A View; frame from Making Memories.

**Miscellaneous, pg. 92**
**Sources:** Card stock, printed paper, stamps, ribbon, buttons, punches, die templates and embossing folder from Stampin' Up!; die-cutting and embossing machine from Sizzix.

**Parenting, pg. 100**
**Sources:** Printed paper from BasicGrey; metallic paper from Die Cuts With A View; stamps from MSE!; distress ink pad from Ranger Industries Inc.; flower brad from K&Company; mask from Heidi Swapp; Design Adhesives leaf from Clearsnap Inc.

**Religious, pg. 106**
**Source:** Card stock, stamps, pearls and punches from Stampin' Up!

**Seasons, pg. 114**
**Sources:** Printed paper from Crate Paper Inc.; stamps from MSE!; brad and rub-on transfer from K&Company; butterfly embellishment from Boutique Trims Inc.

**Sympathy, pg. 120**
**Sources:** Paper from Crate Paper Inc.; chipboard from BasicGrey; stamps from MSE!; paint from Making Memories; ribbon from Fancy Pants Designs; flower from Prima Marketing Inc.; red jewel brad from K&Company; mini brads from Creative Impressions Inc.; Design Adhesives glitter circles and glitter from Clearsnap Inc.; decorative-edge scissors and Cloud 9 Design Rain Dots stickers from Fiskars; heart die and die-cutting machine from AccuCut.

**Thank You, pg. 126**
**Sources:** Card stock, stamp sets, ribbon and pearls from Stampin' Up!; watermark ink pad from Tsukineko LLC.

**Words of Wisdom, pg. 132**
**Sources:** Printed paper from BasicGrey; silver paper from WorldWin Papers; stamps from MSE!; fine-detail ink pad from Tsukineko LLC; ribbon from Creative Impressions Inc.; cord from May Arts; ribbon buckle from Making Memories; Design Adhesives scallop border and glitter from Clearsnap Inc.; punch from Marvy Uchida.

## BUYER'S GUIDE

**AccuCut**
(800) 288-1670
www.accucut.com

**All Natural Accents**
(808) 737-5045
www.allnaturalaccents.com

**American Crafts Inc.**
(801) 226-0747
www.americancrafts.com

**BasicGrey**
(801) 544-1116
www.basicgrey.com

**Boutique Trims Inc.**
(248) 437-2017
www.boutiquetrims.com

**Clearsnap Inc.**
(800) 448-4862
www.clearsnap.com

**The Crafter's Workshop**
(877) 272-3837
www.thecraftersworkshop.com

**Crate Paper Inc.**
(801) 798-8996
www.cratepaper.com

**Creative Impressions Inc.**
(719) 596-4860
www.creativeimpressions.com

**Die Cuts With A View**
(801) 224-6766
www.diecutswithaview.com

**Fancy Pants Designs**
(801) 779-3212
www.fancypantsdesigns.com

**Fiskars**
(866) 348-5661
www.fiskarscrafts.com

**Heidi Swapp**
(904) 482-0092
www.heidiswapp.com

**Hobby Lobby Stores Inc.**
www.hobbylobby.com

**K&Company**
(800) 794-5866
www.kandcompany.com

**Making Memories**
(800) 286-5263
www.makingmemories.com

**Marvy Uchida**
(800) 541-5877
www.marvy.com

**May Arts**
(203) 637-8366
www.mayarts.com

**MSE!**
(719) 260-6001
www.sentiments.com

**Prima Marketing Inc.**
(909) 627-5532
www.primamarketinginc.com

**Ranger Industries Inc.**
(732) 389-3535
www.rangerink.com

**Scenic Route Paper Co.**
(801) 653-1319
www.scenicroutepaper.com

**Sizzix**
(877) 355-4766
www.sizzix.com

**Spellbinders™ Paper Arts**
(888) 547-0400
www.spellbinderspaperarts.com

**Stampin' Up!**
(800) STAMP UP (782-6787)
www.stampinup.com

**Tsukineko LLC**
(800) 769-6633
www.tsukineko.com

**WorldWin Papers**
www.worldwinpapers.com

_The Buyer's Guide listings are provided as a service to our readers and should not be considered an endorsement from this publication._

Our hearts, our prayers, and our love are with you